Photographs and text by George Ancona

Turtle Watch

MACMILLAN PUBLISHING COMPANY NEW YORK   COLLIER MACMILLAN PUBLISHERS LONDON

To Manfred Peters, a friend whose sensitivity and relish of life made this book possible.

TAMAR (Projeto Tartaruga Marinha of the Instituto Brasileiro de Desenvolvimento Flo-restal) is supported by the World Wildlife Fund International, PETROBRÁS, and GRUPO ARACRUZ, and receives administrative support from Fundação Brasileira para Conservação da Natureza and Fundação Garcia D'Avila.

Macmillan Publishing Company
866 Third Avenue, New York, NY 10022
Collier Macmillan Canada, Inc.
First Edition   Printed in the United States of America

10 9 8 7 6 5 4 3 2 1

Design by George Ancona
Map, page 22, by Isabel Ancona
The text of this book is set in 14 pt. ITC Cheltenham Light.
The illustrations are black-and-white photographs.
Library of Congress Cataloging-in-Publication Data
Ancona, George. Turtle watch.
Summary: Text and photographs depict the endangered situation of sea turtles, current efforts to protect them, and the effect of these conservation methods on those people who sell or eat the turtles.
1. Sea turtles—Juvenile literature. 2. Endangered species—Juvenile literature. 3. Wildlife conservation—Juvenile literature. [1. Sea turtles. 2. Turtles. 3. Rare animals. 4. Wildlife conservation] I. Title.
QL666.C5A53   1987   597.92   87-9316   ISBN 0-02-700910-6

Author's note: The arcs in the sky on pages 4-5 are actually stars. They look this way because they moved during a time exposure.

Introduction

After surviving seventy million years of environmental upheaval, sea turtles are on the verge of extinction. These large reptiles, which live in the warmer oceans, must surface to breathe. And during the nesting season, the females leave the protective oceans to lay their eggs on beaches.

Once on the beaches, turtles are easy prey to humans. They are killed and their meat is sold to restaurants. Their calipee, the soft yellow fatty material on the lower shell, is used to make canned turtle soup for export. Their shells are made into jewelry and eyeglass frames. Their skin becomes wallets and shoes. Their oil is used for cosmetics. And their eggs are dug up from sandy nests and sold as a delicacy.

Many nations are now supporting projects to protect turtles and to alert people to their rapid disappearance. One such project is located on a remote beach on the northeast coast of Brazil. It is called TAMAR, which comes from the Portuguese name for sea turtle, *Tartaruga marinha.*

TAMAR is coordinated by Guy and Maria Angela (Neca) Marcovaldi. Also part of the project are Alexandre Filippini and Julio Gonchoroski. The oceanographers live and work in two houses nestled at the foot of a lighthouse on the beach of Praia do Forte.

This book is about their efforts and the effect they have had on the fishermen of the town. It is a story that could be told of the many places where concerned people are striving to save these precious members of our planet, the sea turtles.

Twice every night during the sea turtles' nesting season, a jeep bounces along the beach of Praia do Forte, and a searchlight sweeps the sands between the jeep and the ocean.

Now Neca and Julio are covering the fourteen kilometers of beach. Later Guy and Alexandre will take the second watch.

The oceanographers are looking for the tracks of a sea turtle. The tracks will lead them to a nest, where they may be in time to find a female turtle laying her eggs.

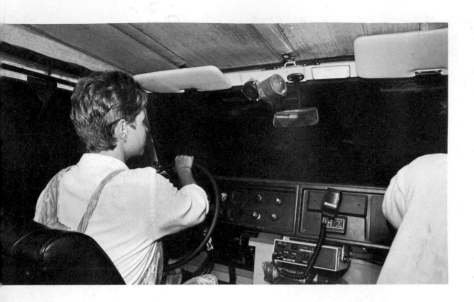

Suddenly, above the roar of the wind and the motor, Julio shouts, *"Tartaruga!"* Neca slams on the brakes and switches off the motor. Dousing the lights, they both jump out into the darkness and scramble silently down the slope to the dark shape on the beach.

While still at a distance, Julio and Neca hear the turtle's flippers scrape the sand. Moving slowly behind the turtle, they turn on a flashlight briefly to see the creature. It is a *Caretta caretta,* or loggerhead turtle. Her shell is encrusted with barnacles. She is building her nest.

The turtle has just finished digging her bed, or body pit, a slight depression in the sand in which she now rests her bulk. She is building her nest above the high-water mark, since saltwater would kill the eggs.

Neca and Julio watch as the turtle begins to dig out the egg cavity. Using her rear flippers, she scoops out a hole in the moist sand. In dry sand, the cavity would collapse.

The turtle raises the front of her body as she works, enabling her to dig a deeper hole. She lifts each flipper full of sand vertically so that she will not disturb the wall of the hole. By now the cavity is about sixteen inches deep. Finally, the turtle widens the bottom of the hole.

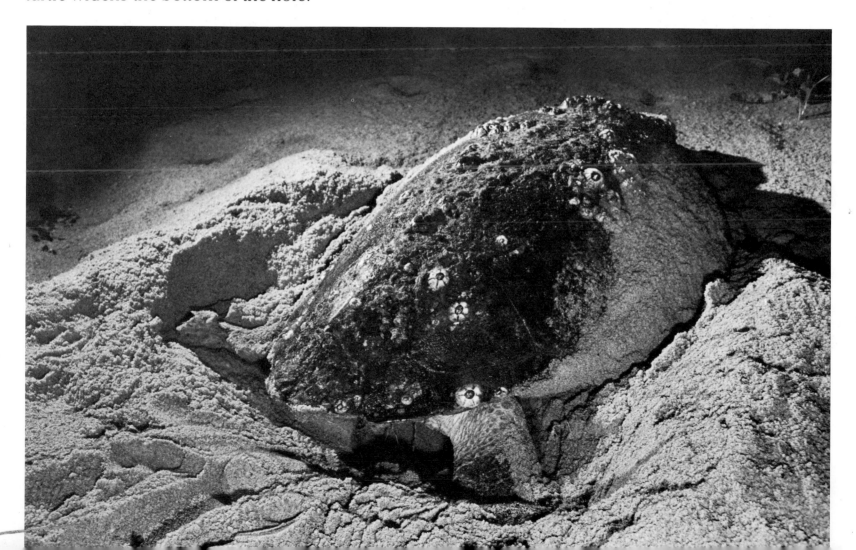

Julio scrapes away some sand beneath the loggerhead to reveal the egg chamber. The cavity completed, the turtle releases a thick liquid from the cloaca, an opening located slightly in front of her tail. This mucous will protect the eggs as they fall and fill the nest.

Now the turtle's body begins to contract, and the first egg drops into the cavity. As the contractions continue, eggs begin to fall at a faster rate. In about twenty minutes, the turtle has laid from one hundred to one hundred and fifty eggs. The eggs are about the size of a Ping-Pong ball, not hard but leathery and flexible.

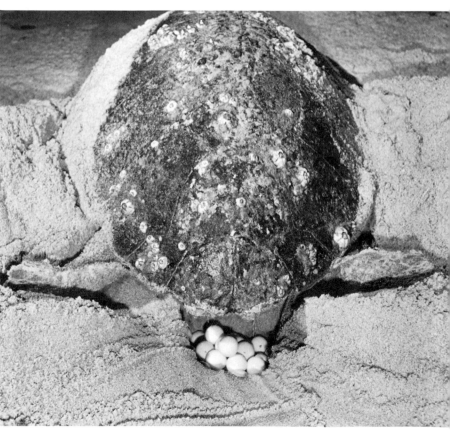

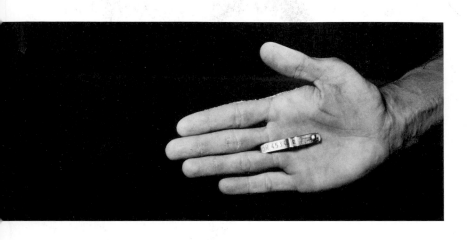

While the turtle is laying her eggs, she seems to be in a trance. She is not disturbed by the camera or by the flashlight that Julio uses from time to time.

Julio moves in to attach a metal tag to the turtle's right front flipper and to measure her shell. The tag carries a number and a request that anyone finding the turtle advise TAMAR of the tag number, the location of the sighting, and the dimension of the shell. From now on, whenever this turtle is seen nesting, scientists will be informed and will learn more about the habits of sea turtles.

While nesting, the turtle has been secreting a liquid from her eyes. Since turtles live in saltwater, they must eliminate salt from their bodies all the time. What they cannot excrete by urine they eliminate through ducts next to their tear ducts. This process also keeps sand out of their eyes while they are nesting. And it has given rise to the popular story that they are crying from the effort of laying eggs.

Using her rear flippers, the loggerhead now begins to bury the eggs. She gathers sand from the side of the bed and sweeps it into the egg cavity until the hole has been filled. Then she moves forward and uses her front flippers to fill in the entire bed. Almost an hour has passed since Neca and Julio first sighted the turtle.

The turtle seems awake now and aware of her surroundings. Breathing heavily, tired from her efforts, she turns around and begins her return to the ocean. The tracks she leaves parallel those she made when she emerged from the sea. When she reaches the water, she hesitates, lifts her head, then plunges into the waves and disappears.

Neca and Julio know that the turtle will be back. They have learned from the tags on other turtles that she will return to this beach to lay eggs as many as three times each nesting season, which lasts from September through March.

Neca and Julio have followed the turtle to the ocean. Now they go back to the nest for the eggs. If they were to leave them, the eggs might be dug up by other people, or by wild dogs or other animals. With a thin stick, Neca and Julio prod the nest to locate the egg cavity. Once they feel a soft spot, they start to dig with their hands. Soon the eggs are uncovered.

Making sure the eggs remain at the angle at which they found them, Neca and Julio count the eggs and put them inside a Styrofoam cooler. Julio packs them in moist sand to protect them during the trip back home. Then Neca measures the depth of the egg cavity.

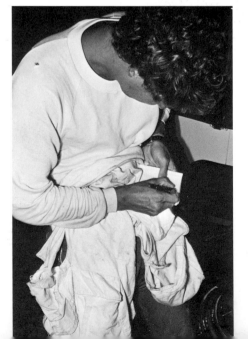

Back at the jeep, Julio makes note of the number assigned to the turtle, its species, the size of its shell, the depth of its nest, and the number of eggs found inside.

Then the scientists return to their base and carefully transfer the eggs to a new nest. They bury the eggs at the same depth at which they found them. There the eggs will be protected from the heat while they incubate for about fifty days.

A metal screen, partially buried, is placed around the new nest. This will keep small animals out and later will keep the hatchlings in.

Sea turtles nest along beaches of tropical and subtropical lands. In the Western Hemisphere, these include the beaches of North, Central, and South America and the islands of the Caribbean. The threat to turtles nesting here has been so great that today six of the hemisphere's seven species of sea turtles are considered endangered.

Praia do Forte

Scientists and conservationists alone cannot save the sea turtles. The people who depend on turtles for their income must help. In the town of Praia do Forte, TAMAR has been working with the fishermen. Guy and Neca have hired those known to be good at finding eggs. The men have been adding to their income by taking eggs to TAMAR. Their children have been growing up with new ideas about turtles.

Two of these children, Flavio and Rosa, have always lived in Praia do Forte. Their father, Everaldo, is a fisherman who is very knowledgeable about turtles. He was one of the first men asked to find eggs for TAMAR.

Flavio and Rosa often roam the beach in
their free time. They also like to visit their
grandfather and hear about his life as a
fisherman, about the time when there were
plenty of turtle eggs to sell and eat. He tells the
children how good the eggs tasted —and how he
misses them.

After leaving their grandfather, the children go out to explore the beach for turtle nests. Flavio wears Grandfather's old hat. Most of the time the nests have been emptied by the oceanographers. But when Rosa sees the remains of a turtle's tracks, the children become excited. Perhaps this nest was made after the jeep finished its last tour of the night. They both begin to poke around in the sand.

Picking up a stick, Flavio and Rosa probe
the sand the way their grandfather taught them.
Sure enough, Rosa feels the stick slip into the
egg cavity. They both begin to dig furiously,
sending the sand flying in all directions.

Soon Flavio cannot reach any deeper, but Rosa, who is bigger, continues to dig. Stretching out her hand, she touches the leathery eggs and shouts with excitement. Then she hands the eggs to Flavio, who places them very carefully inside Grandfather's hat. When the hat is full, the children decide to stop and cover the rest of the eggs.

After covering the nest and marking the spot, Rosa and Flavio run to show their father the eggs. Along the way, they are joined by friends.

When Rosa and Flavio call out to him, their father appears over the side of the boat he is repairing. Flavio holds out the egg-filled hat. Everaldo is pleased that his children are also skilled at finding eggs. He tells them to show Guy and Neca what they have found. The children leave for the lighthouse.

The lighthouse is only a little way up the beach from the fishing boats. The area around it is fenced off. Inside the fence are rows of buried eggs that were found on the beaches. Each nest is surrounded by a mesh fence. There are also three large, round tanks where captive turtles are raised for study. Palm fronds shelter the tanks from the hot tropical sun.

The children are glad to have an excuse to visit the project. And Neca is delighted to see them and to receive the eggs.

Neca takes Rosa and Flavio to the rows of buried eggs. With a posthole digger, she makes a new hole. Rosa sticks her arm out to show Neca how deep the eggs were.

Just as the turtle did, Neca widens the base of the hole. She places the eggs in their new nest and covers them with sand. Then she takes a metal screen and forms a fence around the eggs, burying half of the fence in the sand.

Rosa and Flavio offer to take Neca to the nest where the rest of the eggs are. But before Neca can leave, she must note in a large book the number of eggs she has buried and the place where they were found. She must also assign the nest a number, which is painted on a stick and placed in the nest.

Flavio and Rosa climb into the back of the jeep. The children are thrilled to go for a ride. They bump along the coconut groves at the top of the beach until Rosa points out the site of the nest.

Once Neca has safely packed the rest of the eggs in a Styrofoam cooler and placed them in the jeep, she brings out a long white pole to mark the site of the empty nest. The pole has the same number as the one with the eggs she has buried—14.

Neca tells the children that the eggs will hatch in about fifty days. At that time they can come to see their hatchlings.

Fifty days seems like such a long time to wait. Flavio and Rosa now make regular visits to the turtle pens. Often they wait for their father and the other fishermen to return from fishing. Sometimes little silver fish get stuck in the fishermen's nets. When the men shake out their nets on the beach, the children collect the little fish that fall out. These they take to the turtles in the tanks. Soon they have the turtles coming up to be fed.

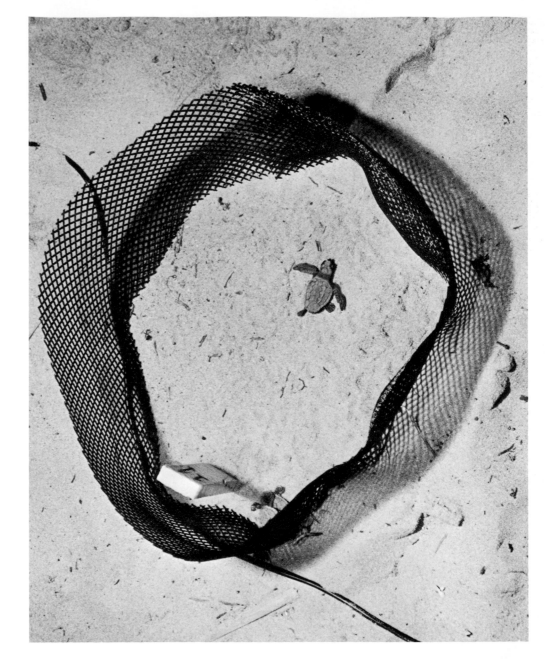

Almost every night, while Rosa and Flavio are sleeping, turtles are hatching. Deep within the egg cavity, baby turtles break through their shells and, working together, burrow their way up through the sand. Soon the first tiny hatchling reaches the surface. It is then joined by dozens of little brothers and sisters.

Turtles prefer to hatch in the cool of the night. They also enjoy the protection of the darkness, which hides them from predators. During the day their tiny black bodies would dry up on the hot sand.

Now time is short. Once the hatchlings are out of their shells, they must hurry to the protective ocean. Neca and Alexandre count the hatchlings, record the number, and place them in a box.

Alexandre drives the hatchlings to the site of their original nest, which is marked by a white numbered pole. There he releases them onto the sand. He wants them to experience the same conditions they would have if they had hatched there. Like little windup toys, their tiny flippers flailing, the hatchlings climb over one another and begin to scramble toward the sea. They are attracted by the luminous waves of the ocean. Alexandre helps them by standing in the shallow water with a flashlight.

Soon the hatchlings reach the white foamy edge of the surf. As they scurry to the safety of the ocean, wave after wave carries them away. When the last little hatchling is swallowed up by the sea, all that is left of them are the tiny tracks on the beach.

It has been fifty-three days since Flavio and Rosa found their eggs. That night Neca sticks her hand inside the nest and feels some movement. Sure enough, later in the night the hatchlings of pen number 14 begin to emerge.

At dawn, Neca goes to fetch Flavio and Rosa. The children hurry to the pen to watch. As the little baby turtles squirm and climb over one another, the children giggle with glee.

Now the sun is getting higher in the sky, and the heat of the day is beginning. Neca says they must hurry. They work together to load the hatchlings into a Styrofoam cooler.

In no time, the jeep takes them to pole number 14, the site of their original nest. Neca puts the box on its side, and the hatchlings make their way instinctively toward the ocean.

Thanks to Rosa and Flavio, who protect them from the birds, all the hatchlings complete their journey—all but one. Rosa picks up this last straggler. Gently she puts it down closer to the water. With the next wave the sea covers her hand, and the last of Rosa and Flavio's hatchlings is gone.

Thanks

To the people of TAMAR, who welcomed me into their lives and work. To Julio and Alexandre, who took me on their nightly travels. To Neca and Guy, who patiently taught me so much.

To Margarida Cintra Gordinho, who guided me through the intricacies of life in Brazil. A most fruitful friendship.

To John L. Behler, curator of the Department of Herpetology at the Bronx Zoo, New York, who was kind enough to review the manuscript.

And last but not least, to Archie Carr, whom I have never met but whose work with turtles these last thirty years has provided inspiration and knowledge to scientists like the people of TAMAR.

Bibliography

Bustard, Robert. *Sea Turtles.* New York: Taplinger Publishing Co., 1973.

Carothers, Andre. "And Then There Were None: The Sea Turtle Tragedy." *The Greenpeace Quarterly,* Vol. 12 No. 1 (January–March 1987): 12–15.

Carr, Archie. *So Excellent a Fishe.* Garden City, NY: Natural History Press, 1967.

Marcovaldi, Maria Angela A. Guagni dei, and Alexandre Filippini. *Projeto Tartaruga Marinha.* Instituto Brasileiro de Desenvolvimento Florestal, 1986.